Table of Contents

God's Divine Plan at Work

Once upon a time, 1600BC, several generations after the family of Joseph had moved to Egypt to survive the famine; the people of Israel had settled in the land and were exceedingly fruitful. They multiplied greatly, increased in numbers, and became so numerous that the land was filled with them.

Then a new king who did not remember Joseph began to rule. He was mean and wicked towards the Israelites. He got jealous about how greatly the Israelites had multiplied so he put slave masters over them to oppress them with harsh work to make the people suffer. They became slaves in the land, but that plan didn't work; because the more they oppressed the Israelites, the more they multiplied!

The wicked king of Egypt then said to some Israelite midwives, "When you are helping one of the pregnant Israelite women during childbirth, if you see the baby is a boy, kill him". How wicked! But the Hebrew midwives were women of God and did not do the evil the king asked them to do. The king then gave the order "Every Hebrew boy that is born you must throw into the Nile but let every girl live."

Now there lived a man and woman, the wife was pregnant and gave birth to a son. The parents were devastated and heartbroken because they did not want to kill their beautiful child; the mother decided to hide him! She did this for three months until she could no longer hide him. One day, she got a basket for him, coated it with tar and pitch to make it float; she placed the baby in the basket and set it along the bank of the Nile River. The baby's older sister stood at a distance to see what would happen to him.

That same day, the wicked Pharoah's daughter went down the Nile to bathe and there she saw the basket with the baby inside! She felt sad for the baby and the little girl who had been watching the baby ran to meet Pharoah's daughter to ask if she would like her to go fetch one of the Hebrew midwives to help take care of the baby. Pharoah's daughter agreed, and the little girl ran to get the baby's mother! The baby was named Moses.

How wonderful to see God's divine work in play. The baby's mother though heartbroken took a step of faith by putting the baby in the basket and setting it on the Nile. She had no idea what would happen to the baby, but she was hopeful, and it paid off. Not only did the baby survive, but she was also able to nurse her child without fear of Pharoah's people hurting him.

God used the wicked ruler's very own daughter to save a child he had ordered to be killed.

What situation are you or your family in right now that seems very sad and difficult? What step of faith can you take today to let God know you trust Him even if you don't know what will happen? Saying a prayer, no matter how long or short is always helpful in times like this. God is always listening so go ahead and tell Him what's wrong.

Moses' Identity, Fears, and Mistakes

Many years after, Moses had grown up; he went out to where the Hebrew people were and watched them suffering from the forced work given to them by the wicked king. He saw an Egyptian beating a Hebrew and he quickly looked around to see if anyone else was watching, and when he saw no one, he killed the Egyptian and buried him. The next day, he saw two Hebrews fighting and he asked them why they were hitting each other. One of the men responded, "Who made you ruler or judge over us, are you thinking of killing me as you killed the Egyptian?" This made Moses very scared as he realized the wrong thing he did, people knew about it.

When Pharoah heard what Moses did, he tried to kill Moses, but Moses ran away quickly. He fled to a foreign land where he lived hidden for many years.

Although Moses was born a Hebrew slave, he was raised in the King's palace. He must have been torn between the two lives. But, it didn't matter his current situation, he did not forget who he was, and he eventually chose to leave behind the things in his life that were separating him from walking in his true identity. Moses eventually did a very bad thing even though he thought it was for a good reason.

Moses made a mistake and chose to run away. *Have you done something wrong, and you feel bad or scared of what might happen if the truth is found out?*

We all have made mistakes, and your mistake is not too big or small for God to forgive. Know this, no matter what, you are loved by those around you and especially by God. Find a grown-up you trust and share the truth with them so they can help you and you can find freedom from the guilt and fear.

For every decision you are about to make, a good question to ask before doing anything is, **what will Jesus do?** We are called to be like Jesus Christ, and He was kind, patient, caring, and obedient. He didn't hurt someone else but instead showed love to those who hurt Him. This didn't make Him weak but instead, a great role model for everyone else to follow. No matter where you find yourself in life, always remember that you are first a child of God. Take some time to thank God for His great love for you and let him know you love Him too.

Moses' Insecurities

After Moses fled from Pharoah, he lived in the desert of Midian for forty years. Moses got married and was one day taking care of the sheep of his father-in-law when the angel of the Lord appeared to him in flames of fire from within a burning bush. Moses saw that though the bush was on fire, it did not burn up. What a miracle! Moses was surprised and went closer to see how this was possible.

When he got closer to the burning bush, the Lord called out to him, "Moses, Moses" and Moses responded, "Here I am". God told him that He had heard the cries and seen the suffering of the Israelites and was going to save them from the wicked Pharoah and his people. God was going to lead them to a beautiful land flowing with milk and honey. God told Moses He was sending him to Pharoah as the person who will deliver the Israelites and bring them out of slavery.

But Moses was scared and responded, "Who am I that I should go to Pharoah and bring the Israelites out of Egypt?". God promised Moses He will be with him. God taught him signs he should perform to make the people believe him and told Moses to tell the people, "I AM has sent me to you". God told Moses to throw the staff in his hand to the floor and it will turn into a snake, God told him to put his hand in his coat and when he took it out, the skin was leprous. As a sign to make the people believe him, God also told Moses to take some water from the Nile and pour it on the ground and it will turn to blood. All these signs Moses did, and it happened as God said.

But still, Moses said to God, "I'm sorry God, I do not speak well, please send someone else". This made God upset with Moses because, despite God showing him proof and promising He would be there with him, Moses felt he wasn't good enough still for the task.

Moses seemed to have been contended hiding, but God had more for him. When God spoke to Moses about using him to deliver the people of Israel, we see Moses make excuses to God as to why not him but someone else.

Have you ever felt like you weren't good enough for a role or task? Has anyone tried to talk you down on something you felt led to do but they tried to discourage you?
Have you been making excuses for fear of failing or what people will say about you?

God wanted to use Moses despite his past mistakes, his running away and him being slow of speech and God wants to use you too. God knew all about all the issues Moses brought up and still chose him. No sin will ever be too great for God to forgive. God has chosen you too, so whatever God is leading you to do, know that He will go with you and make a way for you to achieve it.

If you are unsure of a task or role you are in or about to start, try talking to your parent or pastor about it and have them pray with you for clarity from God. Share any concerns with them and God. God patiently answered Moses' concerns and he will yours too.

Moses Accepts Help and is Encouraged

God refused to give up on Moses as He believed in him even though Moses didn't believe he was capable. So, God suggested Moses' brother, Aaron to help him; letting Moses know his brother was even on his way to him as they spoke. God promised to help them and teach them what to do.

Moses finally agreed to the mission and together with his wife and children, Moses headed back to Egypt. Along the way, the brothers met. Moses told Aaron everything the Lord said and did, and Aaron believed and agreed to help.

Do you ever feel like you need help but are afraid to ask?
What do you think is the reason for that? Fear? Pride? Past hurt?
Do you have a friend you can trust with your plans?
Can your friends and family trust you with their plans?

It's okay to get help and support as you walk in purpose. God appointed Moses' brother, Aaron to be his right-hand man as he led the people out of Egypt. Moses rose to the challenge and together they obeyed and followed God's leading.

God created you to make a difference and he has given you everything you need to achieve it and will continue to do so as you get older. You just need to believe and be willing to do the good He has called you to.

Do not let excuses stop you from doing all the wonderful things God has in store for you. He has also placed friends, sisters, brothers, aunties, uncles, and even your parents to help you. Know you don't have to face challenges alone.

Moses and the Ten Plagues

With newfound courage based on the promises of God, Moses together with his brother approached Pharoah demanding that he let the Israelites go. Moses who once ran from Pharoah out of fear for his life now was standing boldly before him, not just for himself but for all of Israel!

As God knew would happen, when Moses asked Pharoah to let the people go, Pharoah refused and instructed the soldiers to make things even harder for the Israelites. Moses and Aaron performed some of the miracles that God showed Moses such as throwing his staff to the ground and it turning to a snake. But the King of Egypt's magicians performed the same with their evil magic.

One day, God told Moses to meet Pharoah at the river Nile and demand yet again that Pharoah let the Israelites go so they may worship the one true God; Pharoah refused. So, each time the king of Egypt refused, God sent a terrible plague on the people of Egypt.

There was the plague of blood where Moses stretched out his hand with his staff in it over the Nile and all the water in Egypt turned to blood. Yet Pharoah refused, he kept the Israelites as slaves.

Seven days later, Moses stretched out his hand over the streams, canals, and ponds in Egypt and gross frogs came out of them and covered the whole of Egypt! Yet Pharoah refused.

Then the Lord said to Moses, "Stretch out your staff and strike the dust on the ground, and all the dust in Egypt will become gnats". The gnats covered all the people and animals, yet Pharoah refused.

Moses got up early in the morning yet another day to meet Pharoah and ask him to let the Israelites go. When Pharoah refused, Moses sent a swarm of flies all over Egypt! Pharoah was grossed out by this and called Moses saying, "Worship your God here instead", but Moses did not compromise.

Pharoah's heart was still hardened, and he would not let the people go, so a plague on livestock was sent where all the animals of Egyptians died. Yet Pharoah did not care, he refused to let the Israelites go.

Then the Lord said to Moses and Aaron, take a handful of soot and throw it in the air; this soot caused boils all over the people and animals of the Egyptians. Yet Pharoah refused.

Another morning, Moses confronted the wicked Pharoah, asking him to release the Israelites; when Pharoah refused, Moses released the plague of hail over the land. There was lightning and thunder. It was the worst storm in all the land of Egypt. Pharoah tried to trick Moses, lying that if Moses made the hail stop, he would let the people go. But when the hail stopped, Pharoah refused to release them.

Then God told Moses to stretch his hands toward the sky so that darkness spreads over Egypt. He did so and total darkness covered the land. Still, Pharoah tried to play tricks and wouldn't let the people go free.

So, the Lord brought one more plague on Pharoah and all of Egypt. This was the final blow that will make the wicked kind release God's people. At about midnight, all the firstborn sons of every Egyptian died. Finally, the wicked Pharoah agreed to let the people go.

These signs and wonders performed through Moses by God were a way to deliver God's people from the wickedness of a then-great ruler. The people were used as slaves and suffered greatly but God wanted them to have their freedom. God loves His children and is ready to fight on our behalf anything that will try and step in the way of us being free and living the wonderful life God has for us.

Pharoah was selfish and did not care about the Israelites and their suffering. He did not want them to prosper and did not care about the effect his stubbornness had on even his people, the Egyptians.

Is there something you're being stubborn about when deep down you know God is telling you to let go of? Maybe it's anger or unforgiveness towards a friend. Is it bullying or hurt caused by a family member?

God loves you too much and would not harm you, but we are encouraged to always listen to God when He instructs us to forgive, forget or let something go.

Are you trusting God to deliver you, your family, or friends from a difficult situation? Know that whether you can see it or not, God is fighting for you and has your best interest at heart. Keep believing and praying.

The Great Red Sea

The Israelites were happy, they will no longer be slaves! God made the people of Egypt favor them and they gave the Israelites whatever they asked for, food, clothes, gold, you name it.

They journeyed by the desert road toward the red sea, and by day the Lord went ahead of them in a pillar of cloud to guide them on their way, and by night in a pillar of fire to give them light so they could travel by day or night.

When Pharoah heard the Israelites had left, he got angry and changed his mind again. He summoned all his officials and chariots, and they pursued the Israelites, and they overtook them!

When the Israelites saw the great army heading towards them, they were terrified and cried out asking why the Lord brought them out of Egypt only to have them killed in the desert. They complained that it would have been better for them to still be slaves in Egypt than to die out there. They did not trust the Lord despite the great things He did to bring them out of Egypt!

But Moses answered, "Do not be afraid. Stand firm and you will see the deliverance the Lord will bring you today. The Egyptians you see today, you will never see again. The Lord will fight for you, you need only to be still and trust Him".

And Moses cried out to God, and the mighty God told him to raise his staff and stretch it over the sea to divide the water so that the Israelites would walk through on dry ground. Moses did as the Lord commanded him and the Lord drove back the sea with a very strong wind and turned it to dry land for the Israelites to walk on with a wall of water on their right and on their left.

Pharoah and his army saw what happened and tried to chase after the Israelites through the wall of water. Once the last of the Israelites had crossed, Moses stretched out his hand over the sea and it closed, swallowing all the Egyptian army chasing the people of God! The Lord saved the Israelites and the people believed in God and put their trust in Him and in Moses as their leader.

Moses had faith in God when others did not. Despite what the scene in front of Moses was, hundreds of chariots heading his way to harm the people, he believed that God would protect them, and God did.

● ● ●

Faith is the confidence in what we hope for and the assurance about what we do not see. Moses had faith in God, and you can too. Ask God today to help build your trust in Him so whenever you or someone you care about is in a tough situation and it seems there is no way out, you can trust that God will be there with you, and He will protect you.

The Ten Commandments

The people of Israel went on and some months after they left Israel, they got to the desert of Sinai. There, God called Moses up the mountain where God shared many things with him on how to lead the people and how best the Israelites can live. God gave Moses instructions to help the people of God know how to treat themselves and their neighbors right, how to show respect to parents, and how to honor God. These are called the Ten Commandments.

These instructions are so important that God himself wrote them on tablets of stone with his fingers! They are:

1. Worship the one true God and only Him. Do not put anything or anyone else before Him
2. Do not create anything else as a fake god to worship
3. Respect God's name, do not use it in a mean or bad way
4. Remember to take time to rest and focus on God
5. Respect your mother and father
6. Do not kill anyone
7. Married people should always keep their promise to each other to be faithful
8. Do not take what does not belong to you

9. You should not tell lies about other people, always tell the truth
10. Do not compare what you have with another's, be okay and thankful for what you have

The ten commandments were given to help the Israelites live differently from unbelievers, and we as God's children are to live differently as well. We are to show respect to God because we love Him and because He is our Father and Provider. Through loving God, we learn how to love ourselves and others. Jesus summarized all the laws into these two - love God, love others.

Everyone is equal in the eyes of God, and everyone matters. You matter. Your parents' matter, your friends and teachers matter.

Would you like to be treated kindly and with love? Do unto others what you would like to be done to you.

Think of someone who you can show kindness to. It could be that lonely schoolmate or the grumpy neighbor. Your parents need love too even on days they may seem to annoy you the most. Love conquers all, and it starts with you.

Moses' Anger

Now when the people saw Moses was up on the mountain for so long, they got restless and asked Aaron, Moses' right-hand man to give them a new god. Aaron asked them to take off the gold jewelry they had on them. He took what they gave him and made an idol in the shape of a calf. Then he said, "This is your god who brought you out of Egypt". The people began to worship the idol made with human hands and burn sacrifices to it.

Then the Lord said to Moses, "Hurry down now because the people you brought out of Egypt have become corrupt! They have turned away from what is right and true as I have commanded them and made for themselves an idol". God got upset about how stubborn the Israelites were and how quick they were to always grumble and turn to wicked things at the slightest moment of inconvenience.

Moses asked God not to be upset and to not put an end to the Israelites so their enemies will not mock all that God has done for His people. So, God agreed to this. Moses quickly went down the mountain with the two tablets of the commandments in his hands. When he got to the Israelites' camp and saw the idol calf made with human hands and the people dancing and worshipping it, Moses got so angry he flung the tablets to the ground, breaking them. He destroyed the calf and everything the Israelites were using to worship the idol.

Moses was so disappointed about how Aaron let the people get out of control and now were a laughingstock to their enemies.

Moses, just like you and I felt a lot of emotions, some good and some bad. And a lot of times, he acted wrongly based on negative emotions. Aaron his brother unfortunately did not stand firm on what he believed, which is the truth of God, and gave in to the pressure of the people. This caused them to sin greatly.

What do you do when you get angry?
How do you react when those around you get angry?
What do you do when your friends ask you to do what is wrong?
Do you get impatient and make harsh decisions when you're being asked to wait?

Getting angry is not a sin, it is what we do when we get angry that can get us in trouble. James 1:19 – 20 tells us to be quick to listen first, slow to speak, and slower to become angry.

Human anger does not bring out the best that God desires for us.

The next time you're provoked, remember the key question, **what would Jesus do?**

Moses, a Friend of God

The Israelites continued their journey to the promised land and for a bit, Moses met with God outside of the camp in a tent. When Moses entered the tent of meeting, a pillar of cloud would come down and stay at the entrance. The Lord would speak to Moses face to face, as one speaks to a friend.

God is your friend too. He is your father, protector, helper, and guide, and has given you the Holy Spirit to be with you. In the past, not everyone could approach God directly and talk to Him as a friend the way Moses did. But Jesus, the Son of God came down to earth, walked among us, and paid the price for our sins once and for all so we can have a direct relationship with God. Because of this sacrifice, we too are now Children of God and can talk to Him as our very best friend. He loves us, cares for us, and wants us to trust Him with everything in our lives, both big and small.

Ephesians 3:16-17 tells us that God dwells in our hearts so we can talk directly with Him from the moment we receive Jesus into our hearts by faith. It's joyous to know that you don't have to try to win God's love. No amount of good or bad you do will change it. God loves you unconditionally, He loves you way more than you can ever imagine.

If you would like to accept Jesus into your heart and start that friendship with God or have, and want to renew it, you can say this prayer:

Dear God, thank you for sending Jesus to pay the price for my mistakes so that I can be free, forgiven, and have a relationship with you. I accept Jesus into my heart and confess He is my Savior. Thank you that I get to call you my friend and thank you that your word says nothing can ever separate me from your love. Help me to always remember that you are with me on the good and bad days, amen.

May some of Moses' final words in Deuteronomy 31:6 to the Children of God encourage you as well. It says, "Be strong and courageous. Do not be afraid or terrified, for the Lord your God goes with you; He will never leave you nor abandon you."

Here are some bible verses to encourage you as you live boldly for God:

- For I know the plans I have for you," declares the Lord, "plans to prosper you and not to harm you, plans to give you hope and a future. (Jeremiah 29:11)
- Be kind and compassionate to one another, forgiving each other, just as in Christ God forgave you. (Ephesians 4:32)
- So whether you eat or drink or whatever you do, do it all for the glory of God. (1 Corinthians 10:31)
- Jesus replied: "'Love the Lord your God with all your heart and with all your soul and with all your mind.' This is the first and greatest commandment. And the second is like it: 'Love your neighbor as yourself.' (Matthew 22; 37 – 39)
- Don't let anyone look down on you because you are young, but set an example for the believers in speech, in conduct, in love, in faith and in purity. (1 Timothy 4:12)
- As iron sharpens iron, so one person sharpens another (Proverbs 27:17)
- Children, obey your parents in the Lord, for this is right. 'Honor your father and mother' — which is the first commandment with a promise — 'so that it may go well

with you and that you may enjoy long life on the earth. (Ephesians 6:1 – 3)

- If it is possible, as far as it depends on you, live at peace with everyone (Romans 12:18)
- For I am convinced that neither death nor life, neither angels nor demons, neither the present nor the future, nor any powers, neither height nor depth, nor anything else in all creation, will be able to separate us from the love of God that is in Christ Jesus our Lord. (Romans 8:38-39)

Retold by

● ● ●

www.ingramcontent.com/pod-product-compliance
Lightning Source LLC
Chambersburg PA
CBHW041542120626
46551CB00019B/2812